THE GREAT MEANS
OF GRACE

*"And all things whatsoever you
shall ask in prayer, believing, you
shall receive."*

—John 21:22

Jesus is our all-powerful Mediator with His Heavenly Father. He has given us His promise: "If you ask the Father anything in my name, he will give it [to] you." (*John* 16:23). Let us go to Him with unbounded confidence.

PRAYER

THE GREAT MEANS OF GRACE

"Ask, and it shall be given you: seek, and you shall find: knock, and it shall be opened to you. For every one that asketh, receiveth: and he that seeketh, findeth: and to him that knocketh, it shall be opened." —Matthew 7:7-8

"That in all things God may be glorified."
—Holy Rule of St. Benedict

TAN BOOKS AND PUBLISHERS, INC.
Rockford, Illinois 61105

Nihil Obstat: ✠ Stephanus Schappler, O.S.B.
                 Abbas Coadjutor Im. Conceptionis

Imprimatur: ✠ Carolus Hubertus LeBlond
                 Episcopus Sancti Josephi

Originally published at Clyde, Missouri. Eighth edition, 1956, 185,000.

Retypeset and republished in 2002 by TAN Books and Publishers, Inc.

ISBN 0-89555-700-2

Library of Congress Control No: 2001-132393

Cover illustration: Adaptation of details of "Pentecost" window photo. Photo © 1993 Alan Brown, Bardstown, Kentucky. Cover design: Pete Massari, Rockford, Illinois.

Printed and bound in the United States of America.

TAN BOOKS AND PUBLISHERS, INC.
P.O. Box 424
Rockford, Illinois 61105
2002

"All who have been saved were saved through prayer. All who have been lost were lost through their neglect of prayer."

—St. Alphonsus Liguori

(See p. 6)

Contents

PRAYER

THE GREAT MEANS
OF GRACE

"If you abide in me, and my words abide in you, you shall ask whatever you will, and it shall be done unto you."

—John 15:7

Chapter 1

The Excellence and Necessity of Prayer

T. FRANCIS de Sales on one occasion was explaining to some children the happiness of our first parents in paradise. "One of their sweetest joys," he said, "was that Adam and Eve were permitted to walk with God and to speak with Him as to a loving Father." Deeply moved by his reflection, a little boy exclaimed, "Oh, what a pity we can't do the same now! How I would like to speak to God! How I would enjoy walking with Him!"

The holy Bishop smiled at this pathetic utterance and in his winning manner replied: "Be of good cheer, my child. Paradise was lost to us by the first sin, it is true, but **God was not lost to us**. Everywhere He is near us. We may speak and communicate with Him **at all times and wherever we are.** This is done when we pray to Him. In

1

prayer we associate with Him; in prayer we hold sweet communication with God, and God with us, and this converse contains nothing but bliss and happiness."

What an honor it is for us to speak to God, wherever and whenever we wish! This is a privilege we should treasure above all others. "Prayer transforms hearts of flesh into spiritual hearts; tepid hearts into zealous hearts; human hearts into Divine hearts," says St. John Chrysostom. With what reverence, then, should we converse with God!

"Is there anything more excellent than prayer?" asks St. Augustine. "Is there anything more beneficial in our life? anything sweeter to the heart, or anything more sublime in our holy religion? Prayer is the groundwork of all virtues, the ladder by which we mount to God. It is related to the angels, it is the foundation of faith."

"Of all things that we esteem and treasure in this life, there is nothing more precious than prayer," says St. Gregory.

And St. Ephrem exclaims: "Oh, the magnificence and sublimity of prayer! Happy he who prays zealously! Satan cannot approach him, provided he is free from all deceit. Oh, the sublimity of prayer!"

Consoling Words

It is quite true, as St. Augustine says, that man in consequence of his weakness cannot fulfill some of God's commandments by his own strength, but he reassures us in declaring, "So long as God does not deprive you of prayer, He will not withdraw His mercy from you; for He who gives you the spirit of prayer, will give you that for which you are praying. The prayer of the just is the key to Heaven. **In the strength of prayer we are able to do all things.** Prayer is the main protection of our soul. Prayer is the source of all virtues."

"Prayer," asserts Ven. Blosius, "is an impenetrable armor, a secure place of refuge. By prayer alone all evil is warded off from the soul. Prayer purifies the soul, averts the punishment due to sin, supplies for negligences, obtains Divine grace, stifles evil desires, restrains the passions, conquers the enemy, soothes affliction, brings peace, unites man with God, raises him to eternal glory."

"Nothing procures for us such a growth in virtue as frequent prayer, the oft-repeated companionship and familiar relations with God," says St. John Chrysostom.

"By prayer the heart acquires true nobility, it despises the things of the world, unites itself gradually with God and becomes spiritual and holy."

"Great is the efficacy of prayer, for it appeases God, attracts the angels and torments the demons," declares St. Bonaventure.

"Nothing can produce sweeter sentiments than fervent prayer," St. Bernard affirms. "Nothing can fill the heart of man with greater joy, nothing can strengthen him so powerfully to perform heroic deeds and endure sufferings."

The Necessity of Prayer

Whosoever wishes to obtain Heaven must pray. Holy Scripture exhorts us to no other work so frequently as to prayer: "Let nothing hinder thee from praying always." (*Ecclus.* 18:22). "Be prudent therefore and watch in prayers." (*1 Ptr.* 4:7). "Instant in prayer." (*Rom.* 12:12). "By all prayer and supplication, praying at all times in the spirit." (*Eph.* 6:18). And how emphatic are the words of Our Lord that we ". . . ought always to pray, and not to faint." (*Luke* 18:1).

The language of Holy Writ is also the

language of the Saints. St. Alphonsus, in several of his writings, complains bitterly that preachers and confessors speak so seldom of prayer and fail to encourage the faithful in this regard as much as they should. He admonishes them that in their sermons, and while discharging their sacred duties in the confessional, they should be most zealous in impressing upon souls the vital importance of prayer. He wrote of himself, "Every time I preach, I repeat these words: **O people, pray, pray, pray!**"

Whenever the Saints speak of the necessity of prayer, they make use of the strongest expressions and comparisons, as the following statements show:

"Would that I could stand on a high mountain where I could be heard by the whole world. I would constantly cry out: **Pray, pray, pray!**" —St. Teresa of Avila

"As our body cannot live without nourishment, so our soul cannot be kept spiritually alive without prayer."
—St. Augustine

"A fish taken out of the water cannot live; in a very short time it dies. Neither can the soul of man exist without prayer; it will gradually grow languid and die. Let us be convinced that not to pray and to lose the life of the soul, that is, the grace of God, is one and the same thing."

—St. John Chrysostom

"A person who prays will certainly be saved, but a person who does not pray will certainly be lost.* All who have been saved were saved through prayer. All who have been lost were lost through their neglect of prayer."   —St. Alphonsus

---

*Based on the words of Our Lady of Fatima—"Pray, pray very much, and make sacrifices for sinners; for many souls go to Hell because there are none to sacrifice themselves and to pray for them" (August 15, 1917)—may we not hope that salvation is possible even for those who habitually do not pray, if others in their charity make up for this lack? —*Publisher*, 2002.

Chapter 2

Salutary Effects of Prayer

GREAT and glorious are the effects of devout prayer! Prayer moves God to grant us His gifts and graces. **Yes, it constrains Him to do so**, because God is infinitely good and merciful. Our Divine Saviour says, "If you then being evil, know how to give good gifts to your children: how much more will your Father who is in Heaven give good things to them that ask him?" *(Matt.* 7:11).

To inspire us with still greater confidence, Our Lord made this solemn promise: "Ask, and it shall be given you; seek, and you shall find; knock, and it shall be opened to you." *(Luke* 11:9). "All things whatsoever you ask when ye pray, believe that you shall receive; and they shall come unto you." *(Mark* 11:24). "Amen, amen, I say to you, if you ask the Father anything in My Name, He will give it to you." *(John* 16:23). How clear and emphatic are these words spoken by our Divine Saviour!

God **desires** to hear our prayers because He is good; He **must** hear our prayers because He is just and Eternal Truth and has given us His solemn word and promise.

Prayer Obtains the Greatest of Graces, Final Perseverance

The grace of final perseverance is the grace of a good death, a death in the state of Sanctifying Grace. This is the greatest of all graces. A happy death is the end of all evil, the beginning of all bliss.

Saint Augustine observes, "To begin a good work does not mean much, but to **complete** it—therein consists perfection."

"In considering the life of a Christian, a person does not lay so much weight on how he began, but on how he **ended**, whether he persevered. St. Paul began badly, but ended well. Judas, on the contrary, began well, but his end was terrible," comments St. Jerome. "Believe me," says St. Bernard, "Satan is very envious of perseverance, because he knows that perseverance alone will be crowned by God."

The grace of final perseverance is the most necessary of all graces. Our eternal welfare or woe depends upon it. "But he that shall persevere to the end, he shall be saved." (*Matt.* 24:13).

Prayer can obtain for us the grace of final perseverance. This doctrine is taught unanimously by Saints and masters of the spiritual life. All agree with the famous teaching of St. Augustine: "The grace of perseverance can be obtained by humble supplication." The devout and learned Suarez affirms, "If anyone resolutely continues to pray for the grace of perseverance, he will infallibly obtain it."

The illustrious doctor, St. Thomas, writes, "What our merits cannot win, we can obtain by our supplications. **Holiness of life is a fruit of prayer**, but a **holy death is by far more a fruit of prayer.** A person who does not pray for this grace will not obtain it."

"We know," says St. Augustine, "that God grants the grace of final perseverance only to those who ask Him for it."

Although Our Lord had solemnly assured St. Gertrude that she would attain eternal glory, she continued to pray fervently every day for the grace of final perseverance.

Let us consider the words of the learned St. Robert Bellarmine: "It is not sufficient to pray for the grace of final perseverance once or a few times only. We must **continue to pray for it every day**, even to the end of our lives." Let us pray for this grace in the morning, let us pray for it in the evening, at Holy Mass, at Holy Communion, in time of temptation, in time of joy, and Our Lord will assuredly grant us this greatest of all graces.

St. Gregory remarks: "God desires to give us the grace of final perseverance, but at the same time He wishes us to ask for it often, and as it were, force Him to grant it. Without this grace all other graces would avail nothing."

In fact, of what profit would be the most abundant harvest if, in the end, it were destroyed by hail, or washed away by a flood? So, too, what would be the advantage of a virtuous Christian life, without final perseverance? **The grace of final perseverance is an entirely undeserved grace.** No man can claim a right to the grace that will infallibly give him eternal salvation, and strictly speaking, no man can merit this grace. St. Paul says expressly, "So then it is not of him that willeth, nor of him that runneth, but of **God that showeth mercy**." (*Rom.* 9:16).

Final perseverance is neither a reward for our works, nor a fruit of our labors, nor a recompense for our merits. It is a free, gratuitous gift of God's infinite bounty and goodness. We again quote St. Augustine on this subject: "It is the work of God's hands and not our own work, that we do not depart from God." And the Holy Spirit declares in Holy Writ, "I will be merciful to whom it shall please Me." (*Exod.* 33:19).

Prayer Strengthens Us in Time Of Temptation

Prayer is truly a universal remedy. It can be applied to the highest advantage at all times, in all temporal and spiritual necessities. **Prayer is the most excellent weapon to conquer temptations.** Like the Apostles beaten about by the stormy winds of the Sea of Galilee, we cry out in prayer: "Lord, save us, we perish," (*Matt.* 8:25) and the peace and strength of Christ come to our aid in the struggle against the world, the flesh and the devil.

Temptations are necessary for us. "No one can be crowned unless he has conquered," says St. Augustine. Thousands and thousands of temptations are awaiting us on our path through life. We stand in need of thousands and thousands of graces to come forth victorious over Satan. **These graces must be obtained in the first place by prayer.**

"If you ask me," says St. Alphonsus, "by what means you may conquer temptations, I reply: The first means is prayer, the second is prayer, the third is prayer. Were you to ask me a thousand times, I would a thousand times make the same reply." To banish temptations, immediate resistance, profound humility, confidence in God and watchfulness are necessary; but **prayer,** according to the testimony of the Holy Fathers, is by far the most excellent and most efficacious means to win the combat.

Prayer Effects the Conversion Of Sinners

In His boundless mercy God hears the prayer of the sinner and gives him the grace of conversion, for Our Lord says by the mouth of the prophet, "As I live, I desire not the death of the wicked, but that the wicked turn from his way and live." (*Ezech.* 33:11). **It is God's joy and delight**

to grant pardon. How consoling is His merciful assurance: "If your sins be as scarlet, they shall be made as white as snow; and if they be red as crimson, they shall be white as wool." (*Isaias* 1:18). How touching is the well-known parable of the prodigal son. "Father, I have sinned against heaven and before thee!" exclaims the wayward youth; "I am not now worthy to be called thy son." (*Luke* 15:21). His father, full of joy at his return, folds him in his arms and pardons all his guilt.

Again, the publican in deep contrition strikes his breast and says with deepest humility, "O God, be merciful to me, a sinner." (*Luke* 18:13). And behold, he goes forth justified.

Can we find a more tender example of our Saviour's mercy than His dealing with the public sinner, Magdalen? She casts herself at the feet of Jesus. Her lips utter not a word. Her heart is too full for speech. She prays amid tears. Our Lord understands this silent language and speaks the word of pardon, "Thy sins are forgiven thee . . . go in peace." (*Luke* 7:48, 50).

"Two sinners die on the cross at the side of Jesus on Calvary. One prays and is saved, the other does not pray and is lost," observes St. Alphonsus. **Therefore, be comforted, O sinner, and pray.** If you find yourself lacking in courage and confidence, turn to Mary, the Mother of Mercy, the refuge of sinners; with her you will find help.

Prayer Enlightens Our Understanding and Inflames Our Hearts

St. Francis de Sales tells us: "Prayer elevates our understanding unto the light and clearness of God and enkindles our will with the ardor of heavenly love." King Solomon says of himself, "Wherefore I wished, and understanding was given me: and I called upon God, and the spirit of wisdom came upon me." (*Wis.* 7:7).

"I found more wisdom in prayer at the feet of the Crucified," declares St. Thomas, "than in all the books I ever read." This same holy Doctor once asked St. Bonaventure from which book he drew his wonderful learning. St. Bonaventure pointed to the Crucifix with the words: "This is my book; from it I derive my knowledge."

That God's blessing may rest on our works, **all our labors should be com-**

menced with prayer, and with prayer all should be ended. If our work continues for some length of time, we should interrupt it by short, fervent prayers, called ejaculations or **aspirations.** Light and strength will be imparted to our minds and hearts by this holy practice.

"Study without prayer wearies the mind and makes the heart arid," says St. Vincent Ferrer.

Prayer is as the breathing of the loving heart. Without prayer, love cannot exist in the heart for any length of time. **The ardor of love must be enkindled by prayer.**

Very appropriate and worthy of consideration is this comparison of St. John Chrysostom: "In order to keep water warm, it is not sufficient to place it on the fire once only. It must be brought into contact with the heat frequently, in fact, constantly; otherwise it will lose its warmth, will become lukewarm and finally assume its naturally cold temperature. In like manner, our heart must often during the day be replenished by the fire of love in order to retain fervor and pious sentiments; otherwise we will all too soon fall back into our natural state of coldness."

Prayer Obtains Every Virtue

St. Charles Borromeo says that **"Prayer is the beginning, the growth, and the completion of all virtue."**

"Virtues are formed by prayer," says St. Ephrem. "Prayer preserves temperance, suppresses anger, prevents emotions of pride and envy, draws down the Holy Spirit into the soul and raises man to heaven."

By constantly associating with God, we derive grace and strength to practice every virtue. How virtuous and peaceable are those who habitually pray with zeal and devotion! How well pious parents rear their children! How generous such persons are toward the poor, how honest in all their business transactions, how chaste and modest! How frequently they receive Holy Communion, and how zealously they assist at the Sacrifice of the Mass!

Without fear of contradiction we may justly state: **The more and the better a person prays, the better Christian he is.** In a family where prayer is cherished, there is a living Christianity; but where there is no prayer, there is neither Christianity nor true virtue. St. John Chrysostom therefore writes, "If I notice that a person does not love prayer, I know at once that there is nothing good in him. He who does not pray to God is dead and has no true life."

Man is neither better nor worse than is his prayer. To instill into his monks the importance of prayer, St. Bernard was accustomed to say: "Knock at the door of a monastery and inquire whether the spirit of prayer flourishes among its inmates, whether they be zealous at prayer. If you receive the answer 'Yes!' then be assured the monks are holy. However, should you be told 'No!' then depend upon it, their hearts are in a deplorable condition." The same might be asserted of every parish, of every home, of every individual soul. "A person who begins to pray," says a Saint, "ceases to commit sin; but one who stops praying begins to offend God."

St. Lawrence Justinian sums up the effects of prayer in these forcible words: "Prayer transforms men and makes saints of sinners."

We Must Pray in Time of Danger

A child runs to its parents when danger threatens. So should weak, frail man seek aid and protection from God when he is afflicted and tempted. We can scarcely conquer the evil spirits without prayer; therefore, it is our **duty** to pray in time of temptation. This is the doctrine of theologians, and St. Thomas Aquinas declares that **we are bound under pain of sin to pray whenever we are in danger of committing sin**. To trust in one's own strength would be pride and presumption, and in the end such a person would be miserably seduced. God draws by His commandments; the devil entices by his wicked allurements. Whoever does not pray will not obtain the grace of victory, and the devil will triumph.

This is the case especially with temptations against holy chastity. Even good resolutions, the remembrance of Heaven and Hell, are often of little avail, because as St. Alphonsus remarks, sensuality blinds men and takes away their fear of God's punishment. If a person does not pray and take refuge in God when tempted with regard to holy purity, he is lost. The only means of rescue is prayer. Thousands of persons have conquered by praying the **Hail Mary**, or by recommending themselves to the protection of the Mother of

God in these or similar words: "My Queen, my Mother, remember I am thine; keep me, guard me as thy property and possession."

Numberless persons have conquered the most violent temptations because they took refuge in the Sacred Wounds of Our Saviour, embraced the Crucifix, or invoked the Sacred Heart of Jesus.

In bodily dangers, also, as when a heavy cross weighs upon us, or when in danger of death, we must pray; it is our sacred duty. Our Lord desires to aid us, but we must cry to Him for help. In all afflictions Holy Church prays and requests her children to pray. This good Mother summons them to her altars, assembles them before the Blessed Sacrament and prays with them most fervently. Let us imitate her maternal example and pray in all dangers of body and soul.

Prayer Secures God's Blessing On Our Labors

Without exaggeration we can say: Whatsoever is truly great in this world is a fruit of prayer. Every man who has achieved something extraordinary in the Church has been a man of prayer. For this reason the beneficent influence of the contemplative orders in the Church is incalculable. The unthinking world calls such religious idlers, yet they are most useful persons. Christ spent thirty years of His life in prayer and seclusion, and devoted but three years to teaching in public, to show us that the interior, secluded life of prayer is ten times dearer to Him than the active life.

Mary and Joseph, the greatest Saints, led a hidden, interior life of prayer. For the same reason Our Lord said that Mary Magdalen had chosen the "better part" in preference to Martha. This view has ever been held by the Church, for according to the doctrine of the holy Fathers, the contemplative state, the state of prayer, is a necessity for the Church Militant here on earth. This state, above all others, draws down God's blessing on the Church, wins the battles of the Lord and brings about triumphs for His Spouse, the Church.

As in the Church, so in the family. It is a great favor to have God's blessing on our work, on our undertakings. But let us never forget, it is prayer that draws down this blessing on our labors. To have **peace** in the family, to experience **joy** and **comfort** in the children, is a **fruit of prayer.** If our business prospers, if our enterprises succeed, we may owe this to someone who is praying for us, or it may be because we ourselves often kneel down and pray.

Prayer aids us in every necessity of life and gives consolation in affliction. Our Lord invites us, saying, "Call upon me in the day of trouble: I will deliver thee, and thou shalt glorify me." *(Ps.* 49:15). "Come to me, all you that labour, and are burdened, and I will refresh you." *(Matt.* 11:28).

We may also pray for temporal goods, and God will hear our prayer, provided such goods are no obstacle to our attaining salvation. "All things, whatsoever you ask when ye pray, believe that you shall receive, and they shall come to you." *(Mark* 11:24). **Our Lord makes no exception. He includes everything,** temporal favors as well as spiritual graces. In the **Our Father**, He **commands** us to pray for "our daily bread." God hears our petition for temporal goods; this is likewise the doctrine of the infallible Church. Holy Church knows well that man may plant and water, but God must give the increase. For this reason the Church has ordained the Rogation Days, the three days of prayer and procession preceding the Feast of the Ascension [in the traditional Latin liturgy], to obtain God's blessing upon the fruits of the earth.

Yes, God grants petitions for temporal favors. Every Christian may and should, therefore, pray for success in business, for the preservation of health, for a bountiful harvest, etc. We must, however, always pray with conformity to the Will of God. How often has God in His infinite goodness most strikingly granted the requests of those who with childlike confidence prayed to Him for prosperity in temporal affairs!

Why Our Lord Seems Not to Hear Our Prayer at Times

"I have prayed so long but it is all in vain! God will not hear me. My prayer is useless." How frequently we hear expressions of this nature. It is wrong to complain thus. Our prayer is never useless, never in vain, if we pray devoutly. True, our petitions may not always be granted in the manner we desire, but listen to what St. Isidore says: "Frequently God does not grant the prayers of some persons **in the manner they desire,** in order to make them **redound to their salvation.**"

St. John Damascene says very beautifully, **"Not to receive what you desire, often means to receive something better."**

The great theologian St. Thomas Aquinas writes: "God acts like a wise physician, whose patient requests him to take away the medicine, but the physician, knowing how beneficial it is for the sick person, does not remove it. God treats us in the same manner. He does not deliver man from tribulation, even if he begs for this favor, because by patiently bearing it, man can work out his salvation."

"God knows the exact hour when it will be salutary to give us something. The child screams and pleads for the knife; the loving parents, however, refuse to give it. God treats us similarly. He gives us something better than that for which we ask," writes St. John Chrysostom.

St. Gertrude once said to our Saviour, "Why is it, O Lord, that my prayers are so often ineffectual?" Jesus replied, "If I, who am unsearchable Wisdom, occasionally do not answer your prayers according to your desire, it is without doubt in order to give you something more beneficial, because in your human weakness you are not capable of realizing what is most advantageous for you."

In our temporal affairs, especially in trials and tribulations, in sickness and misfortune, we should always pray with resignation to the Will of God.

The prayers of many are not answered because they will not give up mortal sin; because they desecrate their tongue by cursing and blaspheming, or because they do not pray with humility and attention. Alas! How many say their prayers carelessly and without reverence, and thus deserve punishment rather than the grant of their petitions. "A person who prays carelessly," says St. Bernard, "and still expects his prayers to be heard is like a man who pours bad grain into the mill and expects to receive good flour in return."

Whether we pray alone or with others, we should always pray with **humility, devotion** and **becoming reverence.** If we pray in common, it is highly improper to rattle off our prayers as quickly as possible. How many persons give no thought to God as they hastily repeat a certain number of **Our Fathers** or **Hail Marys.** As a rule, it is utterly impossible to have any devotion at such hurried prayers. Those who do not wish to pray slowly, and in an edifying manner, not only rob others who pray with them of the consolation and fruit of devotion, but they rob God of the honor due to Him and deprive themselves of the benefits of devout prayer.

We would never dare to present our petitions in such a hasty, thoughtless manner to an earthly superior, whether in the spiritual or civil order. We would forbid subjects to approach us in such an attitude. How much more should we shrink from addressing God, the Most High, in so irreverent a manner!

Chapter 3

The Meritoriousness
Of Prayer

GREAT and wonderful is the efficacy of prayer! Victory over sin and Satan is gained by prayer; nearly every virtue and grace can be obtained by prayer; the greatest of all graces, that of final perseverance, depends on prayer. In our trials, tribulations and necessities, we should pray to God. Even in temporal matters we should confidently implore His aid. But if the efficacy of prayer is great and wonderful, the **meritoriousness** of prayer is likewise glorious and amazing.

Our Lord Himself teaches that prayer is meritorious when He says, "When thou shalt pray, enter into thy chamber, and having shut the door, pray to thy Father in secret: and thy Father, who seeth in secret, will repay thee." (*Matt.* 6:6).

St. Bonaventure declares, "At any hour

man can gain more by humble prayer than the whole world is able to give him."

However, prayer is meritorious only if performed in the state of Sanctifying Grace and for the love of God, because we can merit nothing for Heaven unless we are in the state of grace. Why? Because he who is in mortal sin has no **union with Christ,** and this is the **principal condition** for acquiring any merit. "As the branch cannot bear fruit of itself unless it abide in the vine, so neither can you, unless you abide in Me." (*John* 15:4). Where love and a good intention are lacking, this relation to God is also wanting. "Without Me, you can do nothing" (*John* 15:5), said our Saviour, that is to say, "nothing meritorious for Heaven."

By prayer we obtain, first, **an increase of Sanctifying Grace**, and secondly, **an increase of glory in Heaven.**

An Increase of Sanctifying Grace

For every good work performed in the state of grace we merit an increase of Sanctifying Grace. Prayer is a good work, a meritorious action, because it includes in itself many virtues. In prayer we offer to God our profound homage and reverence; we praise and magnify the Most High as the King of infinite majesty, as the Creator of Heaven and earth. We join in the thrice repeated "holy" of the angelic spirits. All these acts are exceedingly precious in the eyes of God.

Further, prayer is the practice of faith, hope and charity; the practice of humility, of gratitude, an expression of confidence in and resignation to the Will of God. How many acts of virtue are contained in devout prayer! We may well say that prayer is the most excellent of all good works, because no other good work comprises so many acts of virtue, and by no other good work is God more honored and glorified. If other good works, such as fasting and almsdeeds, effect an increase of Sanctifying Grace, how much more will a devout prayer augment Sanctifying Grace in our souls!

This increase of Sanctifying Grace is an infinitely great gain. Is there anything more precious than the **Blood of Christ?** A single drop of the Precious Blood of our Saviour surpasses in value all the treasures of this world. And this Blood of Christ is the **purchase price of Sanctifying Grace.** The Saints owe their eternal happiness solely and exclusively to the fact that they are in possession of Sanctifying Grace, and the reprobate will eternally suffer dreadful torments on account of the loss of grace.

Ah, how precious is Sanctifying Grace! It makes us children and friends of God, transforms the inmost being of our soul, elevates us to the nobility of Heaven, makes us participators of the Divine nature (*2 Ptr.* 1:4), yea, it verily **deifies us.** This is the sublime reward we merit by prayer. Ought we not to take delight in praying, since the recompense is so infinitely great?

An Increase of Glory in Heaven

By prayer we merit eternal life and an increase of heavenly glory. Prayer, as we have seen above, effects an increase of Sanctifying Grace, and this brings with it an increase of heavenly glory. Sanctifying Grace and heavenly bliss are closely connected. **Our degree of glory in Heaven will correspond exactly to our degree of Sanctifying Grace.** Every degree of Sanctifying Grace will be rewarded by a corresponding degree of glory. In Heaven every one will be rewarded according to his works; each one will be recompensed according to his labors. "He who soweth sparingly, shall also reap sparingly; and he who soweth in blessings, shall also reap blessing." (*2 Cor.* 9:6).

A good prayer always effects an increase of heavenly glory, provided he who prays is in the **state of Sanctifying Grace.** This gain is of unspeakably more value than we can imagine. Even the lowest degree of glory is a treasure of infinite worth. After St. Teresa realized by Divine revelation the great difference in the various degrees of glory and bliss in Heaven, she did not hesitate to affirm: "Were it left to my choice either to suffer every imaginable torture to the End of Time in order thereby to gain one higher degree of glory, or without any trouble and suffering, to possess a somewhat less degree of bliss in Heaven, I would with all my heart prefer to suffer and obtain that degree of beatitude."

What constitutes a higher degree of glory? The essential happiness of the elect consists in the Beatific Vision. In Heaven we shall see God face to face. "The essential bliss of the elect," says St. Thomas Aquinas, "consists in clearly beholding the Divine Being; there is an infinitely great dignity in this vision, and therefore nothing better can exist, just as nothing better than God exists."

St. Francis of Assisi encouraged himself in the midst of trials by saying, "The eternal glory which I expect is so great that I joyfully endure all sufferings, all illness, all calumnies, all persecution, that may come upon me."

St. Vincent Ferrer declared: "The glory of Heaven is so incomprehensible that all the sufferings of this life, yea, all the tortures endured by martyrs, are not a sufficiently great price wherewith to merit, not to say Heaven, but even an hour of heavenly bliss."

"Were it necessary to die a thousand times a day in order to be enrolled in the Book of Life, in order to deserve to see Jesus Christ in His glory," asserts St. John Chrysostom, "a person ought willingly to endure all these torments to become worthy of so great a good."

The Beatific Vision is vouchsafed also to those of the elect who are adorned with the lowest degree of glory. "The last in the kingdom of Heaven will be as bright as the sun, which then will be seven times more lustrous than now," says St. Augustine. A higher degree of glory consists in a higher degree of the knowledge and the love of

God and resemblance to Him. The higher
the degree of glory, the deeper will be the
knowledge, the more intimate the possession, the more tender the love of God, and
the more perfect the resemblance to Him.
**Every additional degree places us
nearer the throne of the most Holy
Trinity.** With every additional degree, our
glory, our joy, our bliss is heightened.

If, then, the very last inhabitant of the
kingdom of Heaven, who is adorned with
but a single ray of light and glory, is sub-
merged in a boundless ocean of bliss and
rapture, how great must be the beatitude
and ecstasy of one who is adorned with ten
thousand degrees of this heavenly glory!

Even a devout prayer, an **Our Father**,
a **Hail Mary**, can increase our future happiness one or more degrees. How many
degrees a person who worthily and lovingly
receives **Holy Communion,** or who assists
at the **Holy Sacrifice of the Mass** in intimate union with our Saviour can gain! In
consideration of these untold advantages,
should we not love to pray, should we not
offer all our actions to God by a good intention, and for love of Him bear patiently all
afflictions and trials of this life?

The Meritoriousness of Prayer

Another Consoling Thought

Let us reflect upon another consoling thought. **Every degree of glory that I merit belongs to me personally.** No one can deprive me of it; by mortal sin alone will it be lost. I can neither give it away nor yield it to another, even should I desire to do so. As the increase of Sanctifying Grace is my merit, so every degree of glory which I have obtained is my own possession.

Saints have gone to Purgatory to expiate their imperfections, and sinners have sometimes been admitted to the joys of Heaven after a short time of suffering in those purifying flames. But the Saint was raised to an immeasurable height of glory while the sinner may have obtained but a few degrees of glory.

What a consolation, what a joy to know that by prayer we can so easily obtain a higher degree of eternal happiness! Everybody is able to pray, not only priests and religious, but also busy fathers, sorely tried mothers, tradesmen and laborers, sons and daughters, children and aged people, those in health and those who are ill—all can pray at every hour of the day and during

the night. One devout aspiration, one act
of resignation to God's holy Will, can
increase Sanctifying Grace and thereby
also augment our heavenly glory.

Love of God and love for our own soul
should urge us to pray often, to pray
devoutly, to pray gladly. Alas, when there
is question of some temporal gain, we
allow ourselves no rest day or night; but
when eternity is concerned, when our
eternal happiness is at stake, how sloth-
ful, how indifferent we are! Were it possible for the Saints in Heaven to suffer
regret, they would grieve bitterly at the
thought that they could so easily have
attained many higher degrees of glory, had
they not carelessly lost the opportunities
while on earth.

However, it is to prayer that the Saints
owe the graces by means of which they have
become Saints. It is by prayer that we too
will be saved and attain to sanctity and a
high degree of divine love.

Oh, let us pray often, let us pray while
we are given time. Let us "Walk whilst you
have the light, that the darkness overtake
you not." (*John* 12:35). Let us heap up treasures for life eternal, for all too soon will
the moment be at hand when for us time

will be no more. For us, too, "the night cometh, when no man can work." (*John* 9:4).

Chapter 4

How We Should Pray

A Sinner Should Pray with a Contrite Heart

A PERSON who is in the state of mortal sin and is not willing to abandon his sinful ways is an enemy of God. To pray effectually, he must have true contrition for his sins and a firm purpose to amend his life. St. Augustine therefore gives this advice: "First we must weep, then pray." "The prayer of an evil tongue," says St. Bonaventure, "is not the supplication of one who prays, but the hissing of a serpent."

"If, however, a person falls into sin through human frailty or rashness," says St. Alphonsus, "and sighs over his misery and desires to be delivered therefrom; if he implores God to rend the fetters of his sins, he may rest assured that God will hear his petitions." Our Lord Himself declares: "For every one that asks, receives" (*Luke* 11:10), be he just or sinner.

St. Augustine asks, "If God did not hear the prayers of the sinner, what would it have availed the publican to ask for mercy?"

"When we pray for graces," says St. Thomas, "it is not absolutely necessary to be already friends of God; prayer itself will make us become His friends."

According to the words of St. John Chrysostom, no contrite sinner has ever implored God's grace and mercy in vain. The words of our Divine Saviour Himself assure us of this: "Come to Me, all you that labor and are burdened, and I will refresh you." (*Matt.* 11:28). Who should come? Only the just [those in the state of grace]? No! "They that are in health need not a physician, but they that are ill." (*Matt.* 9:12).

Consequently, Our Lord's invitation here is meant **particularly for sinners.** The word "burdened" is interpreted by the holy Fathers as referring to sinners who are groaning under the weight of their sins, who take refuge in the Lord in order to be converted and to obtain their salvation. Only the impenitent sinner who continues to live in the state of mortal sin, who loves his sins, will not be heard.

God is so greatly inclined to pardon sinners that He laments their perdition when they depart from Him and live as dead to His grace. How lovingly He calls them, saying, "Why will you die, O house of Israel? . . . Return ye and live." (*Ezech.* 18:31-32). He promises to receive the soul that has forsaken Him as soon as she returns to His friendship: "Turn ye to Me . . . and I will turn to you." (*Zach.* 1:3). Oh, if sinners but knew with what tender mercy God stands waiting to forgive them! "The Lord waiteth, that He may have mercy on you." (*Is.* 30:18).

In a word, He has declared that when a person repents of having offended Him, He forgets all his sins: "I will not remember all his iniquities." (*Ezech.* 18:22). As soon as you have fallen into any fault, raise your eyes to God, make an act of love, and with humble confession hope assuredly for His pardon. Then God, who is "merciful and gracious, patient and of much compassion," will let you hear His words to the penitent Magdalen, "Thy sins are forgiven thee," and He will give you strength to be faithful to Him for the time to come.

If the prayer of the sinner thus pierces the clouds, how acceptable and precious in the sight of the Lord must be the prayer of the just and devout soul!

We Must Pray with Humility

"We must pray with humility," writes St. Bernardine of Siena. "Humility must live in the interior and manifest itself in the exterior; for it would be of little avail exteriorly to bow the head and strike the breast, if he who prayed did not also inwardly bend the spirit and humble himself."

Without humility there is no virtue. Humility is the foundation of all virtues. "God resists the proud, but gives grace to the humble." (*James* 4:6). "A Christian's whole religion consists in humility," declares St. Augustine. This is taught us clearly by Our Lord in His parable of the Pharisee and the Publican.

Everybody loves a humble person, and **God loves the humble prayer of a humble heart.** Such a prayer will certainly be heard. "The prayer of him that humbleth himself shall pierce the clouds . . . and he will not depart till the Most High behold." (*Ecclus.* 35:21). And in the book of *Psalms* we read, "He hath had regard to the prayer of the humble, and He hath not despised

their petition." (*Ps.* 101:18). Even though
we have committed many sins, the words
of the ***Miserere*** will ever remain true: "A
contrite and humbled heart, O God, Thou
wilt not despise." (*Ps.* 50:19).

**The more humbly we pray, the more
certain we are of being heard,** and the
greater will be the graces we receive,
because God is infinitely generous. Our
Lord once revealed to St. Catherine of
Siena: "Know, My daughter, that he who
perseveres in humble supplication for
grace will obtain all virtue." How humble
was the prayer of St. Philip Neri! Every
morning he would make this petition:
"Lord, preserve me this day or I shall
betray Thee."

Even the Son of God humbled Himself
profoundly when, in the Garden of Olives,
He prayed to His Heavenly Father. "And
kneeling down, he prayed." (*Luke* 22:41).
"**He fell on His face,** praying." (*Matt.*
26:39). And this He did three successive
times. When we pray, whether standing or
kneeling, we should reverently fold our
hands and close our eyes or direct them to
the altar. Let us speak to God in a humble, reverent posture, mindful of our Saviour's prayer in Gethsemane.

St. Cæsarius, Bishop of Arles, contemplating Our Lord at prayer, exclaimed: "Mercy supplicates, and wretchedness will not pray! Omnipotence prostrates itself, and wickedness is ashamed to kneel! Sanctity humbles itself to the earth, and wickedness will not deign to fold its hands! The heavenly Physician kneels in the dust and passes whole nights in prayer, and he who is sick will not stoop. Our Judge prays and implores mercy, and he who is guilty will not beg for pardon!"

St. Bernard says, "If it be true that thousands of angels serve the Lord, and ten times a hundred thousand stand before Him—oh, with what reverence and humility should poor wretched man draw near, when he desires to approach this Divine Majesty!"

We ought, indeed, to abase ourselves in the presence of God, but this does not hinder our treating Him with the most tender love and childlike confidence. As St. Alphonsus says, "He is Infinite Majesty; but at the same time He is Infinite Goodness, Infinite Love. In God we possess the Lord most exalted and supreme; but we also have Him who loves us with the greatest possible love. He disdains not, but delights that we

show toward Him that confidence, that
freedom and tenderness which children
show toward their parents."

We Must Pray with Fervor And Recollection

We pray with zeal and fervor if we pray
with our whole heart, our whole soul, with
earnestness and recollection. The eyes must
pray, the lips must pray, the heart must pray,
in a word, our whole being must pray. Holy
Scripture warns us: "Before prayer prepare
thy soul, and be not as a man that tempteth
God." (*Ecclus.* 18:23). And let us hear what
the Saints have to say.

"When we pray, the voice of the heart
must be heard more than that proceeding
from the mouth."   —St. Bonaventure

"It is better to say one 'Our Father' fervently and devoutly than a thousand with
no devotion and full of distraction."
                                    —St. Edmund

"What audacity, yea, what madness, to
turn away our mind and direct our attention to all sorts of folly, while the Divine
Majesty is speaking to us in prayer."
                                    —St. Bernard

"Just as our hands are joined and raised upwards in prayer, so should our lips and our hearts be united."—St. Vincent Ferrer

Prayer should be from the heart, not from the lips alone. Prayer is and must ever be the **work of the soul,** the work of the heart's deepest emotions. "Much love," says St. Augustine, "but not many words, when thou prayest."

We Must Pray with Confidence

God has solemnly promised to hearken to a prayer said with confidence. "All things whatsoever you ask in prayer, **believing,** you shall receive." (*Matt.* 21:22). "All things whatsoever you ask when ye pray, believe that you shall receive, and they shall come to you." (*Mark* 11:24). God is displeased with a want of trust on the part of souls who sincerely love Him and whom He loves infinitely. Therefore, if you desire to please His loving Heart, converse with Him in the future with the greatest confidence and tenderness possible. "I have graven thee in My hands," says Our Lord by the lips of the prophet Isaias (49:16). Beloved soul, He meant to say: What dost thou fear or mistrust? **I have written thee in My hands**

so as never to forget to do thee good.

Whoever prays with faith and confidence may look for success in his cause. Our Lord often revealed to St. Gertrude the delight He takes in a confiding soul, and once said, "A person who prays to Me with full confidence does violence to Me, so that I must grant him whatsoever he requests."

Another time, after having prayed fervently for a certain intention, St. Gertrude asked, "O Lord, what shall I add to these prayers to make them yet more efficacious?" Jesus, turning to her with a countenance full of sweetness, replied, **Confidence alone easily obtains all things!** Confidence was the characteristic feature of St. Gertrude's life, and she was accustomed to say, "All that I have received I owe to my confidence in the gratuitous bounty of my God." The following is another of her revelations, showing how agreeable to Jesus was this confidence. "Although I regard with pleasure," said Our Lord, "all that is done for My glory, such as prayers, fasts, vigils, and other like works of piety, still **the confidence with which the elect have recourse to Me in their weakness touches Me far more sensibly.**"

This same truth our Saviour likewise impressed upon St. Mechtilde: "According to the measure of faith and firm hope with which one expects to receive from My goodness and mercy, so much and **infinitely more** will be given to him; for it is impossible for Me to refuse to man that which with steadfast faith he believes and expects." What consoling words!

Encouraging also is the comment of St. Bernard: "Our confidence determines the measure of the graces that we receive from God. If our confidence is great, we will obtain great graces, for Divine grace is an inexhaustible fountain: whosoever carries thither the vessel of confidence will draw therefrom a great quantity of riches."

St. Augustine says, "How can we fear that our petitions will remain unanswered when Eternal Truth Itself has promised to hear him who asks?" And St. Thomas Aquinas states: "Our confidence in prayer must not support itself on our own merits, but on the mercy of God and the merits of Jesus Christ." According to this same holy Doctor, it is the **confidence** and **not the sanctity** of him who prays that **imparts to prayer its efficacy.**

We Must Pray with Perseverance

For a long time St. Bridget had been tormented by many temptations against holy purity. She implored God fervently to be delivered from these assaults, but in vain. The longer she prayed, the more violent the temptations seemed to become. At length, in a moment of weakness, she exclaimed impatiently, "Behold, O Lord, I have prayed to Thee for years, and Thou wilt not hearken to me! Why should I continue to pray longer? I feel that my supplications have no value in Thine eyes! I will therefore no longer disturb Thee, and my lips shall not open again to pray."

In this spirit of discouragement, Bridget fell asleep. Lo! In a vision the virginal Mother of God appeared to her and asked reprovingly: "What! My daughter, do you wish to give up the practice of prayer? Do you wish to follow the instigations of the wicked enemy and thereby lose the twofold crown of prayer and perseverance? Do you wish to leave the path of virtue and pursue perdition on the road to sin? O daughter, are you not aware that your Bridegroom wished to put you to the test, and are you not willing to endure the trial?" St. Bridget was greatly abashed at these words, and thenceforth continued to pray perseveringly.

How easily we too complain and listen to the deceptive whisperings of the evil spirit: "So often and for so long a time you have prayed; what benefit have you thus derived from your prayers? Cease praying, it is useless; you will never be heard; it is all in vain." Do not listen to the demon, nor complain. Place your trust in the goodness and mercy of God; continue to pray humbly and with confidence, and truly you will not be confounded.

"Ask," St. Augustine admonishes, "ask, and if that for which you plead is not given you, then seek; should that for which you seek be refused to you, very well then, knock." How long a time? Perhaps three months? Take an example from St. Monica, the mother of St. Augustine. Not three months, not three years only, but nearly seven times three years she prayed for her son, until her petition was granted and Augustine was converted. Oftentimes, God does not grant our petitions immediately, in order to increase our merit; for by prayer, Sanctifying Grace is increased, and our glory augmented in Heaven.

The touching words of Our Lord to St. Gertrude on a certain occasion show how He thus mercifully delays an answer for our greater reward. The people in the locality of St. Gertrude's convent were distressed by bad weather. She and her religious had besought God to abate the trial, but perceived no good result from their prayers. The Saint then addressed Our Lord: "How canst Thou for so long a time withstand the wishes of so many persons when I alone have, by my confidence, obtained favors from Thy mercy of far greater value?"

Jesus deigned to make this response: "Would it be surprising if a father let his son ask him a long time for a piece of money, when he had determined to give him a hundred pieces of silver every time he should make the request? Neither should you wonder if I now delay to grant your petition, because as often as you call on Me for assistance by the slightest word or thought, I prepare for you eternal goods which are worth infinitely more than what you ask."

"God wills that we implore Him," says St. Gregory. **"He wills that we compel Him, He wishes to be conquered by importunity."**

Our Saviour Himself teaches us this by a parable: "Which of you shall have a friend, and shall go to him at midnight, and shall say to him: Friend, lend me three loaves, because a friend of mine is come off his journey to me, and I have not what to set before him. And he from within should answer, and say: Trouble me not, the door is now shut, and my children are with me in bed; I cannot rise and give thee. Yet if he shall continue knocking, I say to you, although he will not rise and give him, because he is his friend; yet, because of his importunity, he will rise, and give him as many as he needeth." (*Luke* 11:5-8).

Rightly, therefore, St. Hilary says, "The obtaining of grace depends mostly on **perseverance in prayer.**" Persevering prayer is the key that unlocks all the coffers of heavenly graces, and this key is accessible to everyone.

We Must Pray with Resignation To the Holy Will of God

Our Divine Lord is our most perfect model, not only in all virtues, but also in prayer. We should therefore imitate His actions. In His agony He prayed, "Father,

not My will, but Thine be done." This condition of conformity should never be wanting in our prayers of supplication. Our
Divine Master teaches us to pray in the
Our Father: "Thy will be done on earth
as it is in Heaven."

We read that St. Francis Borgia earnestly
implored God to prolong the life of his
beloved wife who was dangerously ill. As
he was fervently pleading for this favor, a
voice from Heaven sounded in his ear:
"Your wish shall be granted, but it will not
be for your good." Francis burst into tears
and exclaimed, "Thy will be done, O my
God, not mine! If it be pleasing to Thee,
take not only my wife but also my children
and myself." God took his wife and daughter by death; Francis Borgia became a
priest, an illustrious General of the Soci-
ety of Jesus and a Saint.

On one occasion Our Divine Lord
appeared to St. Gertrude, holding in His
right hand health, and in His left, illness.
"My daughter," He said, "choose whichever
you prefer." Which did St. Gertrude choose?
Health? No. Illness? No. Unable of herself
to decide which would be more salutary for
her, she simply replied, "Lord, let Thy will
be done, not mine."

With Jesus in His agony, let us ever seek to pray with perfect resignation: "Father, not My will, but Thine be done."

However, whenever spiritual needs are concerned, for example, to conquer our passions, to obtain pardon for our sins, to make progress in virtue, to obtain an increase in the love of God or the grace of perseverance, we may ask unconditionally. In this case our will cannot be opposed to the Divine Will.

We Must Ask in the Name Of Jesus

The Son of God, by an express promise—we might almost say by a solemn oath—vouched for the granting of our petitions if presented in His Name: "Amen, amen, I say to you, if you ask the Father anything in my name, he will give it to you." (*John* 16:23). By these words our Saviour says to you, "Do not hesitate, go to My Father and present to Him your petitions. It is true, you do not deserve to be heard, but I am deserving; make reference to Me and My merits, and I will support your petition at the throne of My Father."

Trusting in the merits of Christ, we may confidently approach the Heavenly Father in the Name of Jesus and say to Him, "O my God, grant me this petition; look not on my unworthiness, but 'look on the face of thy Christ.' (*Ps*. 83:10). For the sake of the merits of Thy well-beloved Son, for the sake of His bitter Passion and Death, on account of His infinitely Precious Blood shed for me, and on account of His Sacred Wounds, hear me, O good Father!" Will the Father listen to us? Yes, He will. He cannot do otherwise—He must hear His beloved Son.

Oh, how happy are we, children of the Catholic Church, since the merits of Jesus Christ are deposited in the true Church and belong by right to her children. If we appeal to the merits of Jesus Christ and unite our prayer with His prayer, then our prayer becomes the prayer of Christ. **Let us pray in the Name of Jesus.** Holy Church sets the example. She expects everything from God, but only through Jesus. This is why she concludes all her prayers with the words: We beseech Thee through Jesus Christ Thy Son Our Lord, who liveth and reigneth with Thee in the unity of the Holy Ghost, one God, world without end. Amen.

St. Alphonsus Liguori encourages us to this practice, saying: "Let us pray in the Name of Jesus. Let us invoke the Name of Jesus when we are steeped in sufferings;

He will comfort us. In temptation, let us
call upon Jesus; He will give us strength
to resist all our enemies. If our love is cold
and arid, let us invoke Jesus; He will
enkindle our hearts. Happy the souls who
often and devoutly bear this sweet and holy
Name on their lips, a Name of salvation,
a Name of love."

The Church, the Place for Prayer

Although we should pray often and
everywhere, the church is the special place
for prayer, for it is the "House of God." **God
is in the church as in no other place
on earth.** He is there as God and Man in
the most Blessed Sacrament. There He is
enthroned upon His throne of grace, of
mercy and compassion. There He invites us
with inexpressible love and condescension.
Under the lowly appearance of bread He
conceals His greatness and majesty, so that
we may approach Him fearlessly and with
full confidence.

Once the devout Father Alvarez knelt
before the Blessed Sacrament, absorbed in
prayer and meditation. Suddenly he perceived in vision the Child Jesus in the
Sacred Host. The Infant Saviour extended

His arms toward Alvarez, and in His hands there sparkled as many precious pearls and gems as He could hold. At the same time the servant of God heard these words from the lips of Jesus: "If only someone were here to take them from Me."

The church is, indeed, the most suitable place for prayer; in no other place can we pray so well. "My house is the house of prayer" (*Luke* 19:46), says Our Lord. The Real Presence of Jesus Christ in the Tabernacle, the wonderful communication of the holy Angels, the sublime services which dispose one to devotion—all of these instill sweet peace and recollection into the soul. Let us delight in going to the church, not only on Sunday, but as frequently as possible on weekdays. Let us as often as possible assist at the holy Sacrifice of the Mass where Christ offers Himself for us and prays with us to the Heavenly Father. Oh, how excellent, how perfect does our prayer, our sacrifice become, if we have the happiness to communicate devoutly during Holy Mass. What a consolation it will be at the hour of our death! Then we will not need to fear Jesus as Judge; we will know Him well from meeting Him at Holy Mass, at the Communion rail!

The Efficacy of Prayer
Said in Common

Prayer said in common is a public profession of faith, hope and charity. It has the power of unity and is supported by the intercession of our Saviour. Prayer said in common is an image, or an imitation, of the eternal praise and adoration which the Angels and elect offer to God in Heaven. As St. John represents it to us in the *Apocalypse*, all unite in the same praise, and falling down before the throne of the Lamb, all praise God the Almighty, the thrice Holy One. We too, here on earth, before the altar of the Lamb, before the most Holy Eucharist, unite in the "Sanctus, Sanctus, Sanctus." How pleasing to God is this prayer of united hearts!

Prayer recited in common is usually said with more devotion. Solemnity makes a deeper impression. For this reason the Church celebrates her feasts with such splendor. "We therefore assemble on festivals," says St. Vincent Ferrer, "that we may mutually incite each other to devotion, and our prayer thus ascends to God full of love."

Prayer said in common has a powerful efficacy. It is like an onslaught made upon Heaven, a violent assault on the Heart of God. All the faithful call to God and petition Him unanimously, with one voice and one soul. Speaking of prayer in common, Tertullian uses this beautiful simile: "We assemble in great numbers, in order that, like a powerful army, with united strength and one voice, our prayer may be answered. In this manner we force the Almighty, as it were, and do violence to Him. And with such violence He is even pleased." Eternal Truth itself thus testifies to the power of united prayer: "If two of you shall consent upon earth, concerning any thing whatsoever they shall ask, it shall be done to them by my Father who is in heaven. For where there are two or three gathered together in my name, there am I in the midst of them." (*Matt.* 18:19-20).

If the prayer of even two or three is so pleasing to Our Lord that He assures us it will be answered, how much the more will God be inclined to hear the united prayer of hundreds, yes, thousands! On this subject, St. Thomas declares: "It is impossible that the prayer of many will not obtain whatever can possibly be obtained." Even in the natural order we have the maxim: "In unity there is strength."

Chapter 5

The Efficacy of the Our Father

AMONG all vocal prayers there are none more holy, more efficacious or more pleasing to God than the **Our Father** and the **Hail Mary.** The **Our Father** was cherished in the mind of Christ Himself from all eternity; in the bosom of the Godhead it was sanctified, sweetened, imbued with supernatural power, and finally pronounced on earth by His Divine lips. This prayer and no other did Christ teach us and command us to pray when He said: "Thus therefore shall you pray: 'Our Father who art in heaven, hallowed be thy name. . . .'" (*Matt.* 6:9). Verily, the **Our Father** is a written petition which our most powerful Intercessor dictated and which He advised and commanded us to address to His Heavenly Father.

We also have the consolation of knowing

that **whatever we could desire for His honor and for our salvation is contained in the Our Father** and that thereby we can induce the Heavenly Father to grant our request.

Composed Entirely of Divine Words

The **Our Father** is composed entirely of divine words. We may rest assured that not one of these words will be pronounced in vain; for each word devoutly uttered we merit a temporal and an eternal reward.

Now if this petition composed by Christ Himself is presented to the Eternal Father by a person with great confidence, and he implores God so many thousands of times during his life to let His heavenly kingdom come to him, to forgive his trespasses, how could it be possible that the Father of all mercy and the God of all consolation would refuse to grant the request of the humble petitioner? Continue, be faithful in your petitions, and certainly the Heavenly Father will not turn a deaf ear to your entreaties.

A Divine Prayer

When you are about to pray an **Our Father**, be mindful that it is not a human but a Divine prayer composed by God Himself. Endeavor to give due respect to this prayer by saying it with all possible devotion and attention. Do not pray it hastily, but pronounce the words slowly and distinctly. It is by far more pleasing to God and more meritorious for yourself if you say one **Our Father** slowly and fervently, than a great many hurriedly and without devotion.

If you suffer poverty, then repeat with special fervor the words of the **Our Father: "Give us this day our daily bread."** If you have fallen into grievous sin, then say with a deeply contrite heart: **"Forgive us our trespasses."** If you are assailed by temptations, repeat the words: **"Lead us not into temptation."** If you are burdened down with a heavy cross, then say with a heart confident, yet resigned to God's holy Will: **"But deliver us from evil."** If you experience devotion or special consolation at certain words, repeat them as long as these sentiments last and the Holy Spirit operates in you. This is the proper way to say vocal prayers and to make oneself susceptible to and worthy of God's grace.

The Excellence of the Our Father

"How brief in words and how rich in content is the Lord's Prayer! In it is comprised not merely a prayer as it should be, not merely the proper manner of honoring God, but nearly everything that the Lord has taught or ordained. In this prayer is given a brief summary of the holy Gospel. Upon the **Our Father** all other prayers are to be modeled; with it all others are to be sealed." Thus wrote Tertullian in the early centuries of Christianity.

Saints use the most enthusiastic expressions when they speak of the excellence of the **Our Father**.

St. John Chrysostom: "What prayer could be more true before God the Father than that which the Son, who is Truth, uttered with His own lips?"

Blessed Thomas à Kempis: **"The Lord's Prayer** surpasses all the prayers of the Saints; it excels all the loving affections of inspired souls; it comprises all the sayings of the prophets and the sweet words of the

Psalms. Happy he who ponders on the words of the Lord, the golden words of the **Our Father.**"

St. Augustine: "If we pray in the right manner, we can say nothing else but what is contained in **The Lord's Prayer.** The **Our Father** includes in itself the most excellent prayer."

St. Thomas Aquinas: **"The Lord's Prayer** is the most excellent."

Chapter 6

The Loveliness of the Hail Mary

O F all the prayers to the Mother of God, we should pray the **Hail Mary** with special preference, because it is the most pleasing to her and gives her unspeakable joy. As the **Our Father** was composed by Christ, so the **Hail Mary** was given to us by the Most Blessed Trinity. From all eternity it was borne in the bosom of the Triune God, sanctified and sweetened therein, and in time placed on the lips of the Archangel Gabriel.

He who prays the **Hail Mary** utters not a human, a natural prayer, but rather a Divine, a supernatural prayer, a prayer of which every word contains a heavenly power. What prayer could be more pleasing to the Mother of God than that composed in her honor by the Blessed Trinity and transmitted to her by the Angel? By no other prayer has she been so highly honored; never was so much joy and sweetness imparted to her as by the **Hail Mary**, for when she first heard this salutation, she became the Spouse of the Holy Ghost, the Mother of God; and the Most High became incarnate in her bosom.

The Prayer Dearest to Mary

It is plain from Our Lady's words to St. Mechtilde that no prayer is dearer to her than the **Hail Mary.** This Saint once addressed the Mother of God thus during Holy Mass: "O holy Mother of God, were it in my power to greet thee with the sweetest salutation ever conceived by human heart, I would be most happy to do so!"

Instantly, the Blessed Virgin appeared to her with a silver shield on her bosom on which was engraved in letters of gold the **Ave Maria,** and she said, **"No one has yet surpassed this salutation, and no one can salute me with sweeter words than those of the 'Hail Mary,'** with which the Blessed Trinity greeted me. Man can form no idea of the sweetness I experienced when first I heard this salutation."

The rapture that Mary experienced at

the Annunciation is renewed at every devout **Hail Mary**, as was revealed to St. Gertrude. This privileged virgin beheld in a vision, when the **Hail Mary** was chanted at Matins, three streamlets flowing from the Blessed Trinity into the Heart of Mary. (*Revelations of St. Gertrude*, Book 4, Chap. 2). These signified the exceedingly great sweetness which was poured into the Heart of Mary by the adorable Trinity at the Angelic Salutation.

From this you learn, Christian soul, the beauty and value of the **Hail Mary.** Resolve to recite this beautiful prayer whenever possible. When you are going up the stairs, say a **Hail Mary,** as did St. Catherine of Siena. On your way to church or when you go on an errand, say a **Hail Mary.** If you do not wish to say it vocally, say it in your heart, and you will offer a precious gift to the Queen of Heaven.

St. Catherine of Siena always had the pious custom of venerating Mary most zealously with the Angelic Salutation. She recited this greeting whenever she saw a picture of the Mother of God or whenever she commenced some work. Through this practice she obtained the grace of a constant heavenly purity.

The devout Thomas à Kempis often exhorted his disciples: "Salute Mary with the Angelic Salutation, for she delights to hear this heavenly sound. As soon as I address the Blessed Virgin with the words of the Angel, **"Hail Mary,"** the heavens exult, the earth marvels, Satan is put to flight, Hell trembles, joy returns, my heart is inflamed with holy devotion. Yes, I feel such consolation in my heart that I am not capable of expressing it in words."

We can understand how the renowned Suarez was willing to exchange his works for a single **Hail Mary** devoutly prayed. What are the grandest labors of genius side by side with this sublime summary of the glories of Mary, dictated by God Himself? In saying the **Hail Mary** piously we share in its treasures of light and love.

Preaching in the presence of many theologians, Blessed Alanus proved definitely that **every word of the "Ave Maria" is a jewel** and that he who recites it devoutly offers many gems to the Heavenly Mother.

Since every word of the **Hail Mary** is a jewel, endeavor to pronounce each word with fervor and devotion, that you may be able to present your dear Mother with gems of most precious value. Oh, how great will be her love for you if daily you offer her so many priceless jewels! If we wish to love Mary sincerely, we must begin to pray the **Hail Mary** with true devotion. Then we too may hope to experience the fulfillment of St. Bonaventure's words: "Mary always salutes us with some grace whenever we salute her with a **Hail Mary.**"

Chapter 7

Exhortation

S T. Alphonsus wrote a treatise on prayer containing this forcible admonition, which is well suited for the conclusion of our little work:

"Among all the spiritual works I have published, the treatise on prayer is certainly the most beneficial for the faithful, because **prayer is an indispensable and certain means to obtain eternal happiness and all necessary graces.** I wish it were possible for me to have as many copies of it printed as there are Christians on earth, in order that I could give one to each, and all without exception might realize how important it is to pray in order to be saved.

"This absolute necessity of prayer is explained in all holy books and is clearly and emphatically recommended by the Fathers of the Church. At the same time **I know that the faithful are neglecting**

this powerful means of salvation. I especially deplore the fact that preachers and confessors do not speak more on this subject, and that spiritual books, even those most widely circulated, do not insist on it sufficiently, although there is nothing that ought to be more deeply impressed on the people than the necessity of prayer.

"Let us then be wholly penetrated by the importance of prayer, because, as a rule, all the adults who enter Heaven are saved only by this means. May everyone who desires to be saved apply himself to prayer with more zeal, *for prayer is the key to the treasures of God!* Alas, how many unfortunate souls lose the grace of God, commit sin and finally **lose Heaven, because they do not pray** and ask God for the necessary assistance!"